D0297672

*Southern
Messenger
Poets*

DAVE SMITH, EDITOR

DOING LUCRETIUS

DOING LUCRETIUS

poems • s i d n e y   b u r r i s

Louisiana State University Press   *Baton Rouge*)|(MM

For Nancy, *fairest creature*
and Samuel, *our increase*

Copyright © 1990, 1992, 1993, 1994, 1995, 1999, 2000 by Sidney Burris
All rights reserved
Manufactured in the United States of America
First printing

09   08   07   06   05   04   03   02   01   00
5   4   3   2   1

Library of Congress Cataloging-in-Publication Data

Burris, Sidney, 1953–
    Doing Lucretius : poems / Sidney Burris.
        p.   cm. — (Southern messenger poets)
    ISBN 0-8071-2550-4 (alk. paper) — ISBN 0-8071-2551-2 (pbk. : alk. paper)
    I. Title. II. Series.

  PS3552.U7437 D6 2000
  811'.54—dc21
                                                                    00-020698

The author gratefully acknowledges the editors of the following periodicals, in which some
of the poems herein first appeared, sometimes in slightly different form: *Connecticut Review,
Illinois Poetry Review, Kentucky Poetry Review, Poetry, Sewanee Theological Review,
Shenandoah, Southern Review, Virginia Quarterly Review,* and *Verse.*
    "Strong's Winter" also appeared in *The Best American Poetry 1996.*

Thanks to Nicola, who cast the necessary and cold eye on the manuscript, and as ever,
to Dave, always and all ways.

The paper in this book meets the guidelines for permanence and durability of the Committee
on Production Guidelines for Book Longevity of the Council on Library Resources. ∞

The mother hen has almost lost by disuse the power of flight.
—Charles Darwin

To have fled and to have never seen her face.
—*Chester Mystery Plays,* "The Shepherd"

I have abandoned myself to flights.
—Walt Whitman

I tell you folks, I think I'm leavin'.
—Cowboy Junkies

The sea looked and fled.
—Psalm 114

Fly this place.
—*King Lear*

CONTENTS

I   SUPERNAL YOUTH

It is supernal what a youth can take
& barely notice or be bothered by
which to him older would work ruin.

—John Berryman, "Down & Back"

AFTER RAIN, A WALK THROUGH TREDEGAR

A cloud-broken sun cleavered the rubble, where
four years the unslakable fire of a nation
smoldered, where now we spoke, you and I,
of our modern lives. The river ran smoothly
by those crumbling furnace rooms, and still we loved
two women for the future they held
in their eyes. Pitched black and headlong
behind us, our shadows grew more and more
abstract until you couldn't tell one
from the other. Had we come this far only
to look back, a last chance to make a monument
of a moment? That's how we get along, you and I,
walking through Tredegar,
with the habits of our burdened glance.

THE PATRIOT TREE

And in those days, I was broken from dreams
on hard, white mornings to whip the thickets,

flush a bird or two, and drop
before the shot sizzled by overhead.

Midday, we'd crest a hill
crowned with the Albemarle pippins

King George so loved, it's said
he took his taxes from the trees—

a cue ball of an apple still growing free
on shaggy limbs no one had pruned for years.

A country then with forgotten groves of gamey fruit—
you'd poke the big blade of a jackknife

below its rusted skin, twist,
and up popped a white chip,

a severed tang, with the sound
of parchment crisply ripping.

It lay on the tongue like hoarfrost,
its aftertaste sour and defiant. . . .

Its seeds were hard as flint,
and the grass below as dry as tinder.

KING OF THE BREAKERS

We'd peel our jeans in a flash and up
came the clammy trunks that shrunk a boy's smallness
even smaller—August on the Outer Banks
was burning everything in sight, still,

over the blistered road, barefoot and high-stepping
in time, *ouch-ouch, ouch-ouch, ouch-ouch,*
until we hit the dunes and drove toward the top,
ankle-deep, mired, and working hard,

a pilgrim's progress through sea oats
that rasped and sawed at sunburnt skin . . .
but this was the good penance when suddenly,
over the top, there came a vision—green water,

and an open stride, gobbling yards of sand downhill
to the tidal flat, where the sprint began, each of us
in the water now, arms and legs flailing,
and at the breakers, look left, right,

to know our place in this world, and knowing
our place, know too the sweet abandon
when a gang of spindly boys
get in over their heads, deeper

and deeper until at last with nothing left to do,
the one who will soon call himself king of the breakers
dives with stamina for this kind of living
headfirst into a hard fist of water.

A REALM OF PROBABILITY

For they shall soon wither like the grass.
—Psalm 37

When I was a little boy with little
else to do, I sat down on the long-grass face
of the world that ran through my yard,
saw the world's hard diversity thrashing
about me, and on that day decided
that anything I could possibly conceive
(within a realm of probability
logical to a world without end)
I might just as well go ahead and believe
had probably happened to someone
somewhere at one time or another.
The Pyramids, the Sphinx, the holy gardens hung
with such care, these were textbook wonders
sprung from the perfectly reasonable urge
to serve and be served, and were no wonders at all,
at least not to me and certainly not then,
crouched on the verge of amazements
that seemed now to pop up everywhere:
old Mrs. Crenshaw's chrysanthemums, their gold
and umber deeply darkening in the cold,
her bronze planters holding these fireballs
on either side of her stoop; her dying too
of something that rattled in her throat
with a voice of its own just below her whisper:
Come back tomorrow when I'm feeling fine.
Even then I sensed the way of her speech
was the way of the world: the trees, the faces
of loved ones I saw in the grass, all came
fully in season, and all came to pass.

ANTHEM

There was an anthem when I was young, and it was called "Free Bird,"
and the band that made this anthem was called Lynyrd Skynyrd,

and what it has in common with great art I cannot say,
although when this song kicks off you can hear hounds bay

that are really guitars, and since in my life I heard hounds
cross the mountain ridge in the glitter of fall, and since belief

in God and country then was a belief in the blood that kicked
and thrummed on those days when the world seemed fit

for nothing less than knees-down adoration, so "Free Bird,"
one of the anthems I know word for word,

comes to speak eventually of defiance; of all the dogs
my grandfather turned loose on those days, the one he still brings

up when his mind clears is the one who never came back.
So now I have a new cipher for living: the flight of a gargantuan buck,

how it gave an old man solace in his bed, and how it shows me the
    way to run
for joy in the face of those things I've done, and those I've left undone.

UNDER THE LEARNING TREE

No one survives the hard skies of heaven. . . .
A boy, I looked up, and saw this, and felt
a fragile thing come into my life.
As it came, I knew it was the child
we'd gathered to lay to rest
midsummer as sun-shards fell around us.

On that day, I heard it said she would live in our hearts,
but having no heart for the dead, having never seen the light
the dead are said to bear, I stood clear,
shunted aside by this child,
and it was no passing cloud, it was fragility I saw
darken the faces of those who loved her, it was

old heads on fallow shoulders, as shadows slashed
and mocked the black crepe that flowed from the one wreath,
and these were the shadows that fell from grievers
who now were full of unburdening.
But you cannot tell a griever's shadow
from those who have suddenly come upon joy,

and as our faces settled above our dark coats,
gradually, from one to another, this child passed, who once was joy.
For now, though, joy lay slain in the grass.
But what were we to know,
standing side by side, hand in hand,
as if we held earth's dominion in our magic circle?

We stood to our task.
It would be our common labor,
grieving so harsh as this.
That is what I hoped when this fragility,
once a child, came into my life
under the learning tree where trembling shade
set the ground of summer to trembling.

STRONG'S WINTER

When I hear it said of gods and great literature
that they will never die,
a cowered boy comes to mind
who carried the name Len Strong and seemed proud the day
he watched the snow fall in the schoolyard and said that God did
    not exist,
that he did not care whether Virgil spelled his name with an *e* or an *i;*
and now I want Len Strong to say whether the heavens and poetry
faded for him over the years, an unsleeping retreat,
or whether one night the pressing cold had pressed enough
and Len Strong woke in his winter and knew at once what he would do.

It is said of snow as it falls
that it makes the world a solitary place,
and when Len Strong broke his silence, I could not see
that a schoolyard where solitude came down from the sky
would become in this world a larger thing than God's or poetry's death.
So under the stars above I would ask of Len Strong
that he lead me back
through the schoolyard and into the aching classroom,
that he sit in the last place I saw him
and speak of the solitude we cannot escape.

Across a snow-driven street, I would know Len Strong's lean slouch:
he walked at odds with the angles of the earth.
I would follow him through the whiteness
that grows in increments and wrecks the landscape.
It is what the living call snow, this wreckage,
and when it fell quietly from the sky one winter,
Len Strong shouldered the death of God and poetry,
which nowadays weighs little to me because of this cowered boy
who walked away and lay down one night, leaving
in my life the sharp report of a solitary schoolyard.

LATE AFTERNOON, I RECALL MY FATHER

Seventeen hundred hours. Time for gin
and bitters, 1943, somewhere
in Africa I've only seen captured

by the grim verisimilitude
of the black-and-white photos my father
kept stashed in his deep cache of relics.

In this one, his thong-tough legs have taken him
to Love–30, break and match point, the sun
above, he used to say, the real smasher.

He's been gone now a dozen warlike years.
And left behind a fatherhood
of prancing and swagger:

in that stance, crouched and swaying, a squint
leaves its lines on his coppered face,
and I see him for the first time

as the R.A.F. pilot, hungover still
in his starched whites, must have seen him
from the clay desert of the server's court—

he's dead calm, except for the tremble
that gives him away, the fisted volley
of a lunging man's will to return.

RIVER AND BARN

1.

Day's nearly gone and green's the color
you'd take back
were you here with me
in this place long gone to seed.

Still, what of a springhouse, long afternoons,
where the water's clarity, its cutting coldness
on the tongue, have dredged up
the grandest lie in the world?

I could tell you where there was a fence line,
could say now, no horses, no heifers, only the ghost
of a road gagged with upstart pine.
Better though to say it's all green where I once lived.

But the river nearby, the river I want to tell you about,
that is a different story.
Let this river be
the one that carved caverns in the cliffs that could not hold it,

where, beside that river, summer's dryness hard on the land,
we held each other, you and I,
and made of ourselves a moment we'd never let go.
This then is the river we know.

2.

And what did I know in those days about the fullness of time?
A gabled barn beside a loud river, Saturday nights
when a fiddler sawed his music, and truth, for those who'd have it,
showed up in the backseats of love-worn heaps, radios sputtering

our modern music, the good news from a bad generation.
They were good in their day too, our mothers and fathers,
I know this now about the fullness of time
because forever it is said, *What's gone is gone,*

or *Home's where the heart is,* and all the while the razorlight
of stars rains down on us without mercy as it rained on them.
But the heart's home is of its own making,
that is what I learned when I caught the flash

of the fiddler's puddled eye, clear and pagan,
and it said, *Boy, this world's running down,*
so that night near ceaseless water,
we danced in a barn, arm in arm,

and let the bourbon burn our tongues,
round and round, living for the last song
when the hunger for motion seemed so bred in the bone,
it is the hunger I've come in my life to call home.

HOW TO READ AMERICAN POETRY

Here's one by Frost
about direction, the kind
Rand McNally avoids
because to make up the way
and imagine ordeals
preparing our citizens
for dreamy cities
brings too much to bear
on what we lose
if we disagree:
a way of going together
all of us may share.
Still, it's precise enough
how the poet's imperative
mood orders the storied places
he sees and wants us
so badly to find
that he'll flatter his readers
by calling the others
the *wrong ones* who can't
get the goblet none
of them know they need—
that's a graced bravery,
to set off, arrive
somewhere you've designed,
and return evangelical,
without a word heretical
in the eyes of old New England.

THE DEATH OF TRUMAN CAPOTE

Laid out in my amniotic bath, hot
when I began with Truman, but now
that *Handcarved Coffins* is done, cool as rain.
The water slugs down the drain, leaving me
corpus delicti on porcelain, the flesh
and bones of an unimaginable act
of creation—but you trusted the alliance
between art and death, it gave you phrases,
it gave you vision and the Blue River,
a dark ribbon weaving, you said, through the hands
of the wading murderer.
                            My fierce towel
cannot scrape away the chill. There is evidence
of the cinched rope in your writing fist, that knot
of fingers that governed what you wrote.

OR

1.

Thick slabs of pink light latticed through the porch
on afternoons when a roostertail of grass
arced from a pushmower chirring across the yard;
or the crystal glass, with its classic accent
of lemon; or the voices that seemed to float
in nervous suspension when the lace curtain
trembled by the window; or through the trees
from the church nearby, the big psalm that came
rolling on Saturdays, practice-day for the choir:
once, the demonstrably sacred lay everywhere,
or so I thought, and I believed in animals,
their dominion, lounging on the plains
and hovering over the mesas, resident
in the outcrops and steep cliff faces . . .

2.

but once, I sat where silent Pound said he sat
by the oily waters of the Grand Canal
when he made his unforgettable gambit,
and I had friends back home who'd made a life
from moments like these, casting lots for the splendor
here and now or banking on the joy ever after . . .
at any rate, from where I sat that day, there was
a finely deckled edge to all I saw,
a massive consequence in every line of sight.
But I was done with that animal
innocence, and the wide eyes, the repose
in pastures that has made America famous.
Our youth, it was an old story even then,
and one that I would never tell again.

II   DOMESTIC

Home . . .
> *I should have called it*
Something you somehow haven't to deserve.

—Robert Frost, "The Death of the Hired Man"

DOMESTIC

Our hobbled cat watches an early robin
maraud the fresh-turned soil,

its chitchat a heresy
to him here in our quiet

alcove baffled by snow.
Late winter exacts its humility.

If I'd seen this place in another life
I'd call it austere:

the swallows stitching
their shaggy nests

into crannies that age
the sheer face of the stone wall,

the neighbor's roof mossed over,
his yard rutted by rain,

but here is home,
a domain remarkable

mainly for its light
and reasonable demand

that we go on living
where our old impresario

of the instinct pounces,
wide again of his mark.

BOURBON SONG

Another day, then, spilling buckets
of frothy sunshine
for the cat on the windowsill, and breeze
enough to belly out the curtains,
and just enough unreasonable faith to take
the clouds at their word that they are here
and soon gone because the world, at least the world
from where I sit and rock and drink, the world
is buoyant as a kite when it wants to be,
but a leaden place too is what I learn
when I rise from my chair and sigh the way
I used to feel that grown-ups sighed when they
were just about to say a simple thing
I ought never to forget about people
who spent a lot of money, or believed
too much in themselves, or spoke out of turn—
and hearing myself sigh just such a sigh
and feeling the terrible determinism
of having sighed like a grown-up, I tuck my wisdom
away wherever things like that get tucked,
and feel the shudder wisdom can't dispel,
or won't, a notion I think will come to something
profound, but then that thought, unlike a bourbon,
leads to no other, so I sit back down,
content to nurse the ice in my glass, resigned
to the chill on the hand that grips it.

THE DEATH OF HENRY DAVID THOREAU

The letter-perfect limpid description
never strayed from its master.
Hammering weather forged your tensile lines,
but our summer's been too mild for that.

A moth with a face like an owl lands
on my crumbly Thoreau, waits for its likeness
to pass, then jumps it,

                        and they ram midair,

while others ferris-wheel madly, or zigzag.
They speckle my deck, these flying sparks.
The mild day is burning with perfect wings.

But you're a winter animal now, bad
on committees, no abolitionist.

It was I and the fire that lived there, you wrote.

The snows of heaven drive us from our hearths.

My house is not empty, though I am gone.

ARRANGING PASSION

That brazen day
riddled through and through with sun:
even Dickinson would've told it straight.

A spectrum of flowers,
trimmed stalks, stalks
stuffed in galvanized buckets

of spring water,
buckets hung from tipsy stalls,
coffee cans full of change—

commerce and country
come to town.
                        The beautiful
small profit, small but sure,

of a knock-down,
drag-out, year-by-year love . . .
What else is there for a marriage

to declare? Flowers
in vases have been our buoy,
a splash in heat-sick rooms.

Without them,
only the colored leaves
that show their veins

as they dry, or cicadas
to rattle us a diversion.
Something to arrange,

something our own?
Those lilies I remember,
one by one, that lasted a week.

THE COMPENSATION

1.

Yellow spring erupts from forsythia,

and we've come to count on its interruption:
a tremor in the curtain
shakes sun on the floor,
the light's lace-combed, dancing,
and our bedroom's alive again.
Undercover, we fumble, compensate.

Last night, our neighbors announced their increase,
a nearly perfect child
the whole street'll cherish.
She's more than anyone alone could love.

But I'm glad you stayed with me today;
we've ministered another fine Sunday mess.
Are you cold? The bedspread's lost somewhere
under the rifled paper and china plates.

2.

For once,
it might have served as well,
a postcard from Toledo,
but a taut print instead
gathers the whiteness
of our wall
and attracts it, with clouds,
to the center of the city
suspended in the gilded frame above our bed.

Someday we'll jump up and go there
to see ourselves
if the last plank of Sunday light
rots away in Spain as it rots away here.

3.

Good things of day begin to droop and drowse.

4.

Incumbent, unconcerned to mend our ways,
we're bric-a-brac on pastoral hills
of pillows. Four, five, six . . .
It's late to be here.
Through the bone
sycamore, the season comes whistling.

The alarm clock
hasn't worked for a week.

But we're done with the mawed future. . . .

A run
of days tapered
to elongated El Greco nights

conforms to our wishes
when the horoscopes do not,
and we'll take our pleasure from that.

POSTCARD FROM ENGLAND

A postcard from England emblazoned
with the print of a painting, announcing
an exhibit that featured a friend I'd known
a long time ago, landed on our stoop,
the card worn a bit by its passage,
the painting's title tucked away on back:

Ship of Fools, Trumpeters, 1991.
And in this ship, eight players crowded
together as if in a tub, their postures
suggesting they played to beat the band
with trumpets that were yellow, and red caps,
and their skies could not have been bluer.

How wise my faraway friend has grown since last
I saw him scarfed in mauve, and I must thank him,
and give him this: here, on an otherwise dull afternoon,
I was handed a boatload of men who play
a glorious and silent song, by a postman
who says, *I'm sorry, but it's all I've got today.*

for Thomas Newbolt

TO A READER OF MYSTERIES

*. . . a species of popular fiction which bears much the
same relation to the world of actual crime as does
pastoral poetry to the realities of rural economy.*
—Michael Innes

A better reader than I would call it quits now.
The stiff's in the bag, gut-shot, toe-tagged,
chilled down, and ID'd—his final grimace
still lingers long after his pain skipped town.

But given my druthers, I want a body,
or its sweet-sick odor,
somewhere, in some form, on page one:
here is a world where it's no paradox
that death's the best beginning.

And now friends ought to cross friends for prizes
they covet. A beautiful pair of gams,
a prime tract of land, or simple revenge
will do, and then comes the satisfaction
of watching the desperate grow
inexorably more desperate until
a bad day at the office breaks their will,
and they return to their lofts and begin
to plan the awful demise.

Pebbles and slingshots, or shoves down stairs
are good ways to go, but too English.

There must also be the false trails criss-
crossing our mystical American days
even when lived in a mundane manner,
as here on my deck, watching titmice feed,
I'm an easy whack for a passing assassin:
SHOT DEAD WHILE WATCHING BIRDS, the headlines
would read, and the authorities are baffled.
And what about those birds? A strange fixation?

So why is it soon as the culprit's revealed
there's always part of me wants to read
the book backward, watching the tenuous thread
of solution start to come unraveled,
tracking the bullet as it backs from the wound
and snuggles its way into the barrel,
the wound miraculously healing, while the body found
nearby resurrects the mystery that gave it
its prominent place on page one?

Reason and justice carry us forward
from the glossy cover to the blurbed back,
but the good reader knows that murder and greed
will never be laid to rest beside the bums
stacked in cold storage down at the morgue—
that's an old problem for young philosophers
who must admit at least how right it seems
to begin with a stiff that enshrines
our abiding inability
to gaze into the face of a foggy night
and ever figure who done it.

in memoriam, Howard Nemerov

AN ANTIPASTORAL FOR FRIENDS
MOVING TO THE COUNTRY

Unsympathetic to much of your talk
about the land, even your mid-life need
to go there, or as you said, go *back* there,
we perched ourselves with two dogs and a boy
midtown in a battered house that's old enough
to boast of surviving mess after mess,
both federal and state. The plague of wars
that pocked the century, doing this or that
to whatever tycoon prospered or decayed,
these rooms have outlived; the wavy bubbled glass
in the weighted windows distorts the life
the neighbors lead, and led, long before we came,
and if structures, as architects claim,
embody a way of looking at the world,
then I have no idea what my cellar,
scooped out, rocked in, and dank as a corpse,
would say about its dark resignation
to a netherland where no one expects
to be suddenly glad they've arrived:
nothing's homey about this part of home.
Yet other friends in the country report
(I'll pass this bit of wisdom on to you)
that cellars out there are something to see,
lightless places where potatoes won't sprout
all winter long, where jams and preserves belong,
where a summer's work slumbers under blankets
of snow.
               From here, of course, the morning view
reveals the incomprehensible crowd
we've become: the ancient monsignor across
the way is stooping for his paper flung
while he slept from a suicidal Honda
that could wake the dead peopling his prayers.
And worse, we've no horizon to speak of,
just ill-planned peaks and leaning chimneys
to sketch our notion of a skyline, and stars

no longer umbrella our well lit world;
yet as I lean from my window and survey
the inexplicable projects my neighbor
takes up and abandons in his yard,
or as I look to the golden Hilton
and downtown tenements zigzagged by fire escapes,
I know my neighbors are watching me as if
we'd sprung from one of Bruegel's scenes
where someone peeking around a corner
is being observed by someone above
who's just about to suffer a disaster
of cataclysmic dimension, and all
are convinced they've pulled off their peeps
with a kind of impunity, at least.

Back to the land? Maybe it's just too late;
I mean, what I've read of Arcadia I can't
possibly equal by living there, so here
with our dogs and a boy we gambol up
the stairs to the highest room in the house
to play on a painted floor until the street
lamp sputters and burns, and we watch
the landscape sparkle in common particularity,
as our neighbors' lamps, one by one, follow suit.

for Ash and Kim Nichols

TO A FRIEND IN HMP MAZE

1989

The skies of Arkansas are not so blue
as your ROYAL MAIL censored aerogramme that came
impressed between *The New Yorker* and Lands' End.
Elizabeth's marmoreal profile, embossed
a long inch above my address, peers west.

My dull Buck tatters her prim border.

"Well here at the moment there is little
new. Not really surprising.
                              This year
marks the 20th anniversary
of the arrival of British troops."

No subjects are born subjects, the poet
and tyrant know.

                    You ask about our weather?

Knuckled vines are height-drunk and choke
the trees we know the frost will free.

KING OF SEASONS

Shower-logged sweet gums douse the road red
while squadrons of geese veer southward, home
to a new season, dragging their dumb shadow
through cloud-breaks with the glassy strength
of figurines—they fly to a form kerneled
in the pith of their brains. Others,
unlike them, remain behind and podge through gaunt stalks
our garden left behind.

                    Judgment is soft now,

walking outside after green sheets of rain
quicken the leaning shed,
its odor of rot rich as Croesus,
its century-old strap hinges, its moss-backed
studs and curled shingles holding shape,
then crumbling under my inquisitive touch.

OCTOBER INTERVAL

Just once I intend to be of a mind
to see the world as the world wants
to be seen on a day like today:
a perfectly garish one in October
when the blued skies and dyed leaves beg
to be done up in prose, verse, or casual chat.

"It's crisp! It's brisk! It's weather for sweaters!"—
Here's the blessed interval when we go happily along,
raising our words without malice above
all the odds and ends of an irritable day,
refusing our scripted lives
as we pop through the necks of our mothballed sweaters

and break some kind of summer cocoon—
we've found more things to do today
of an order higher than the grinding tasks
that just confronted us yesterday,
and feeling born to joy, we stop and say,
"It's crisp! It's brisk! It's weather for sweaters!"

SUDDENLY, MONARCHS

Suddenly, monarchs
shuttling through gaunt trees,
on the move, mindful of nothing, zig-
zagging, a pulse of nerves on the air
as if to canopy us from the bleaching sun had been their calling;
but they gave no shelter, they kept no families from harm
though a hard millennium spun to its end.
                                    And what they gave,

the once-in-a-lifetime distraction,
they gave only to those
who would lift up their eyes
and chase a glimmer in this shaded world,
a high party of wings
frail against the lead-gray sky of another autumn grinding by.

And to think I in my sorrow
had believed for a moment they were only falling leaves.
Had believed enough in my life not to lift up my eyes.
Had believed enough not to see butterflies rampaging the trees.

Hordes of them I remember as if they came from the steppes of Asia,
and from centuries ago too
when such beauty gave birth to the bloodlust of nations. . . .

Suddenly then I saw a nation of monarchs riding over my house,
they made no fanfare I could hear,
they showed themselves only in the simple guise of leaves,
and they fluttered but did not return to the ground
as do the things of this earth,
they did not spoil the brief season lovers make and annihilate,
they did not whisper by the windows of bedrooms
where mothers lay their children down for a night of porcelain dreams.

They passed over, beyond all this.

It was an upward motion in the rush of so many falling leaves that
    made me look.

A motion exacting no revenge, no allegiance, only my love
of vanishing things, that is what it took,
an aristocracy of the eye,
and a quicksilver comfort came of it as I saw beyond sorrow
those trees of twitching monarchs.

But as they disappeared
and the trees once again resumed their high emptiness in the air,
there would be multitudes who would hear rumors of this once-in-
    a-lifetime fullness,
and for them, lucky in their way,
sorrow would always be a passing thing,
but for those of us who happened to lift up our eyes on this day,
sorrow was no rumor
because sorrow for us in this world
would now and forever be
a migration of monarchs.

VINCENT VAN GOGH

Assuming the sun to be a knit ball
of umber wool, and the sky wrapped around it
a blue gauze, and the earth below oppressed
by the whole sky-flung apparatus,

he must have suffered hard things when he looked up,
or down, or in, and heard that private command
to paint the face of the world as everyone
in one mood or another

has heard it; but fearing these moments
alone under thick daubs of sun
with sloppy splotches of flower everywhere,
he saw too a bit of heaven fresh fallen,

a fitness that composed him
and ordered the angles and accidents
of his nightmare into the light
of our dying and manageable day.

THE CELEBRATION

Long ago, worms burrowed their characters
into deal planks

I lopped off for this table
to saw bread

without a cutting board,
to slosh liquor

without a care, to spill our song
with no burden—

to live in the handsome air outside the city.
Such a celebration

Bruegel painted, the art
of living art

as if art's enough.
Each of us

a museum of opinions, we stoop
to eat

over the worm-script, the stark hieroglyphic
we ignore

at our peril, and at our peril
have chosen to do so:

muscadine hangs in clumps, a full-bearded vine,
and we tip our cups.

III   MORNING SENTENCES

Sunrise is multiplied,
Like the earth on which it shines,
By the eyes that open on it,
Even dead eyes,
As red is multiplied by the leaves of the trees.

—Wallace Stevens, "Three Travelers Watch a Sunrise"

MORNING SENTENCES

1. Proverb

Dawn. And half-light. Proverbial,
        Encroaching, it'll soon be all
                Over this ordinary kitchen

Where I sat down at sunrise
        To write a thing about fullness
                And time and the holiness

Of waiting. But having waited
        Now all morning long and seen
                The light arrive in feather-falls

On a bowl of fruit,
        What came to mind
                Was a boy I once knew

With a face ghosted
        By his splendid version of Virgil—
                Len Strong he was well named,

And *I sing of a rampant empire*
        Was how he did line one. . . .
                His sibylline grin, such liberties,

Even for the high-school Latin ace,
        Got him after-school detention
                For disrespect and more:

A misdirected object wedged
        Willfully out of place.
                And now, half-light or not,

And having had nothing
        To do with empires
                Except through Virgil's scheming,

Still, I scan the near terrain:
    Sun-slope on rusted pears,
        An unnecessary candle

Burning down like a passed love,
    A knife and fork crossed
        On a single china plate, Len gone.

Sacrifice sifts into this life
    Like light on pears.
        Quietly. Inevitably.

Even the half-light of a proverb would work wonders now.

2. *Under Lilacs*

So much free-fall in late summer:
    leaf-curl, husk of cicada clutching bare limb,
        hard pods gored of their seed by the season's onslaught . . .
      bounty's litter.

It's a wonder we survive the scythe at all.

Flash-point memory: Green Mountains, Vermont,
    and the several arts of our survival on display.

One renegade star, and we marked it, and saw
    the first blush of sunrise, with lilacs,
        their sick sweetness like an oracle, a cave-voice:

You cannot have it both ways.
    Expect no miracle on earth.
      The dead scent in the air
        is the scent of decision,

Then, indiscriminate pink, a sky full of it, and loss,
    and everywhere, vast, marching columns of sunlight.

It dawns on me now I never saw you again.
    Such concord between heaven and earth. . . .

Ever notice, you said, the little thresholds all around us?
    An evening's encroachment,
      the sundial's sweeping shadow,
         Hamlet's transformation?

To step through the world's feigning,
    you wondered, and not be held accountable,
      to live in unpatterned places,
        can we do that?

Leaving is what we do, parting is such sweet sacrament,
    and sacrament, free-falling through the veil, is our survival.

3. *Rise and Fall*

Rome gives ample scope for moralizing
On the vicissitudes of fortune, said Gibbon.
Said I: What place does not?
Particularly if I read *fortune* as *snow.*

A night-long blue falling. By morning,
The storm has lumbered off and garrisoned all I see.
It could have been a lifetime, it happened so gradually.
Instead, someone I loved slipped away.

The slow encroachment of sunlight on white, early
As I sit here, sleepless and emptied, knowing
Full well the snow will vanish today.
Fortune, yes, as *snow,* I read.

4. Lodestar

How unlike himself he'd become, glazed
By new light that first March morning he woke to white lace:
Dogwood, jonquil, lily. And absence
Discovered there, brooding and fertile, mundane as a thumb,
And as necessary too.
But note:
That March morning, first of all mornings, there were song-stylings
    in the air.
That day, he said, *was a dark lodestar.*
Now he'd gone and named it.
And will dredge it up whenever need be.
As now. She, gone.
Lodestar.

The massive pride of desire . . .
Shuck it.

5. Declaration of Independence

I cannot bend a spoon by looking at it, and wishing it bent.
I cannot bend a sightline around a corner. Accordingly,
I cannot know what lies around a corner.

The Kadampa masters of the past had nothing to enjoy in their dry caves.
They said: *Why should we care where we sicken and die?*
And: *We should prefer to die in a bare and empty cave like a bird, a dog,*
         a rat.

I can always tell November by the stub light of morning.
Lessened, diminished.
I say: *It pries into my room, a cave, a mouth, a carnage.*

And how. Flog, flog, flog, flog.
Huddled away, I am doing November now, and the rain November brings.
It will call me out, this falling from clouds, this intercessor,

And I will stand up and go, wet-spangled in the new world.
Or not. That too might lie around the corner. It is not a matter of belief
         making it so.
Crouch and sight, bank, follow your line. Go.

6. *Upstairs, Where I Was a Boy*

I was five but knew enough to know
Mornings would never be the same the night
A passing storm laid our sycamore low.

Unbroken sun though my window,
I woke to an emphasis
Of clarity and realm. A winnowing

Of shadows. And no half-light.
Even the ladder-back rocker
Was all business, Shaker-like.

Mornings in that room: flushed out, revealed, riven.
A world either here or there.
(The pans of a scale, the birth of decision.)

I would take the woman I love back to that room.
And say: *In my beginning there was, How will you know what to do?*
And she: *It's well I know what you're running from.*

7. An Evening by Degas

It is hardly ever morning in a painting by Degas.
Simply—he took away the early downfall of light and found the lateness
    of the world.
The lateness, we had seen it so many times before
And mistaken it for weariness,
Or melancholy, and all the time it was only lateness.
Nothing more, nothing less.
The grandly banal.
Some, looking westward, even called it wisdom, but it was only lateness.
Go and see it in the footlit face of a dancer who bows before a dimmed
    audience,
Performance over, effort dwindling now, another century done
In pastels and halftones.
A ravishing lateness.

It is the stark perspective
You and I share, stranded before this canvas,
Stone-struck to silence, hand in hand, as the gallery closes
And another evening by Degas begins.

8. *Blues for Richard Hooker*

Measure and proportion
Perfect all things.
Everything is for some end,
Though as far as measure and proportion are concerned,
Excess opposes them both.
And nothing perishes except through excess.
So it follows that measure and proportion likewise preserve all things.

And further, whenever we rise
Above ourselves,
Which we do on occasion,
It is not a matter of excess: such is our substance,
So then is our presence.
This would be our fondest hope,
Though often it's true that all our love's in vain.

For example, here now
At this table,
Sunlight spreads its cape
Over a bowl of fruit, a sentence of limitation and restraint.
Do you see?
A morning's worth of sentences,
And the world's pretty well tied down, cinched up, convicted,

And mostly the work got done,
With satisfaction.
Except that in failure
Lies the happiness of freedom when nothing's left to lose.
So much has gone
Untold at this table that I know
A sentence now to be a diminishment, willed

And necessary, but a diminishment
All the same.
So much got away
And never left a trace. Godspeed.

But regard it
From every angle and you too will love
These remains, as I do: a bowl of fruit centered on a table with sunlight.

So call it this,
Only this,
Call it a plain
And sensible token to know
All those things
That we cannot see.
The *verie* truth. Call it this. I do. Godspeed.

IV WAR AND PASSION

Two forms of destiny: war [and] passion.
MADNESS in both cases (cf. Agamemnon).

—Simone Weil, *Pre-War Notebook*

DOING LUCRETIUS

Colossal Mary Frick my senior year
in college could do Lucretius better

than Professor Richardson
had ever seen.

He said so in class
when Mary faltered, when she had to confess

that yesterday her father left home for good,
that through the night-long despair she heard

in the sound of the wind
kicking up cyclones of leaves around

the yard the old Roman grief
creep over the sill and settle in the crease

of her text. And how do you English that?
She couldn't do it

the way it ought to be done
unless he'd allow her the kind of translation

that unpacked
its bags—I quote—*in a grimly determined dialect*

of the heart.
The rest of us figured she'd lost her trot.

But then she began her recitation, and cypress
plus a funeral spray of eucalyptus

came up again and again
as she'd pause to explain

the downward pull of life, how it worked
against the buoyant lift of lyric

like sin and death,
and how this influenced the truth

Lucretian-style: when the plague
came to Athens, the afflicted would beg

to die after a week of black bowels
and nosebleeds. And some leapt headlong into wells

to slake the fever. Bodies were piled
on bodies and laid side by side on a field

of bodies that covered
the field of those who died

a month ago. But even in lurid detail,
Mary's Lucretius couldn't tell

the whole story of desertion, how lives were quick
to go up in smoke,

how families, rather than abandon the body
to unsacred decay,

would brawl to burn
a loved one.

And so sadness came out of the blue
to colossal Mary Frick, who knew

late last night (the old Roman grief propping her up
on the back stoop

where she saw car lights
fading down the street)

that never again would her father call this haven
home.

ULYSSES CRIES

A seascape again, and quite a view.
Off the port side, which common sense said was west,
nothing but the slick sheen of distance, and he loved that best,
always had, because after what he'd been through,
to see a gently rolling wide open space
made him feel instantly a part of it all,
pitched beyond the cluttered detail
of his battering home. And then he wept, and weeping, found solace.

The adoring dolphins that arced in his wake
were not the occasion for his tears,
but something with an otherworldly weight . . .
it was the view off the port side where the moon leers,
that is what caused his tears, and the blank face of water,
and the mute stars, and their unrelenting order.

LEAVE-TAKING

1. *Desire and Flight in a Maritime Museum*

It is something found in maritime museums
everywhere, this willing of motion,
and if you pass an afternoon wandering
room to room where canvas after canvas
seems bloodshot with a sailor's fear of the doldrums,
you might just find the history of your soul
hung on the wall in the wide open air.
Here's one, for example, you'll recognize:
a deep harbor's laid out in the background,
a good ship's just docked there, and you'd cut
and run, given half a chance, because this wide world
looms just over the shoulder of a woman
who knows in her way
what you will know soon enough—
that you have avoided her eyes
for the last time, and now are staring
into the paint-bright oceans
you just discovered were always reflected there.

2. Circe

A handsome sea.
Long bars of light plundered the water . . .
or that's how I recall it.
The ocean pitched fistfuls of spray, they opened in air
and were diamonds, falling.
As the sun in its colossal path crisscrossed the sky,
shadows leaned from our bodies and stretched toward heavy-laden trees:
fig, olive, pomegranate, and under them the blue shade
we avoided, Ulysses and I, that last afternoon.
Such a beautiful sight to see: with the taste of salt
on our tongues, I watched the old Greek decorum die.

Then, he left.
And the island settled down to its tired order.
Diamonds occasionally, and fruit clustered.
Blue shade fell from trees, water pawed the shore.
Love's miracle lasted a good long day
and left a burning I'd kindle for years.
Yet I know a thing now I never knew before;
it flies in the face of the heavens,
and I feel it in the earliest hours of the morning
when I wake to a dawn sky still pricked by stars,
and see them vanish, and see that fire now will have its day.

Noon crackles.
Cicadas chatter back and forth; no sails break the horizon.
My shadow shortens, vanishes into my body
as I stand here inspecting the shipless sea.
For days on end I have fallen to sleep without the ghost
of a chance of his returning.
He prows the water,
that is my certain knowledge, and as he arcs away,
I have come to know another thing too,
that although I can cut a squall down in its prime
or turn men to swine,
I have had a lonesome way of loving the world with my magic,
and I turn my back on all such seeming now

and sing like a woman
who casts no shadow, who sees
that Ulysses will sail to hell and back
and not find my likeness ever again in this world.

3. Ulysses in Hell

So looking back now, I see what Circe said
—*go first to the place of dusky poplars*
and visit the nations of the pale dead—

should've warned me not to trust the words that love
makes, to bring more to a ravishing face
than a pair of eyes that blink and believe,

but still I took to the open sea
with a lone ship and a fit crew
of faithful souls who'd never deserted me,

and we sailed to strange stars if we sailed at night:
the cold and winking fires that once marked
our course had long dropped out of sight.

Then the sea took us down, and we left no trace.

after Dante, Inferno, Canto 26, ll. 100 ff.

4. *Skipping Stones*

At dusk, the water's face lay so still
you could skip a stone across the pond, shore
to shore, and find it perched on the far bank.
The good ones were palm-sized and nearly flat,
but with heft enough to stay the course.
The periodic touching down and taking off
I envied for its easy dalliance
between lightness and weight, like body and soul,
for its being in a place that was no place
in my known world.
It struck to the heart of perfection.
For the moment, integrity was a trail
of dimpled circles that rippled and died.
And best of all was when you found the one
that made it to the other shore,
and its underside was wet as water,
its topside untouched, and high and dry as air.

5. Siren

Enter the pilgrim, a lover now whose journey's an act
of attrition so artful I'd view his death
simply as a self-consuming artifact,

complete unto itself, ancient, a work of art:
he's dreaming now just before dawn of a woman
who does not have a woman's heart,

and as the sun begins to rise, she warms
to his penetrating gaze and sings,
and in her song there is loveliness in swarms

of nectared bees, in lanky flocks of pastel birds,
in lime trees beside the green sea—it is all
too much, he begins to feel, for words

when suddenly Virgil, disciplinarian, magic
man for an empire, tramps into his dream
and rips the shirt off the Siren's back.

A Roman act of exposure: that odor, bile,
the Siren's belly swollen and oozing . . .
the scene could not have been more terrible,

it shook him, it broke his dream,
and he woke at the foot of his master,
who had been calling and calling his name.

after Dante, Purgatory, *Canto 19, ll. 7–33*

6. *Beyond Cádiz*

Once again, the pilgrim, nearing heaven, on a roll:

*I'd climbed so high the universe seemed to smile
and I could see all around,
even to Cádiz and beyond, where the roil*

*of the sea that took Ulysses from us
had settled down, as if in the stillness of water
there is ending. And in ending, peace.*

after Dante, Paradise, *Canto 27, ll. 82–4*

THE WATERFALL

Something godly in the rising
mist of the waterfall
made us wonder
about the spirit's flight
at the end of life,
an old-fashioned thing
for you and me to do,
but we did it anyway.

Only for a moment though
because I knew there'd come
a time the sun would break
a bank of clouds, and brightness
make a momentary heaven
of earth that ordinary day
when all our thoughts concerned
things that last and things

that pass away. Still,
an old-fashioned art,
this talk of spirits and heaven
and bodies lighter than air.
It didn't do us any harm.
Something in the falls
brought us back down to earth,
where I found you in my arms,

listening to the stern crash
of water, and how it spoke
of wisdom and said,
thrive in your cranny
and learn to love
this odd state of affairs
where you fall and fall, and still
never arrive anywhere.

VANISHING POINT

1.

I'd had it explained a hundred times
and been shown as many examples: the point
at which parallel lines drawn in perspective
converge (sometimes through a cloud), well,
that's the vanishing point of the picture.
To find it, some cock their heads and squint,
but I'm told the more professional way
is to follow the gradual diminution
of the figures on the canvas before you,
follow them to the point of their vanishing
and oddly enough you've found the thing you sought.

2.

The example I remember was a scratched slide
of a Madonna and Child whose vanishing point
lay high on a white mountain that rose
far beyond the manger where the birth
that was not a birth had just taken place.
Already the nimbus glowed softly.
"Look to the snowy peak," my instructor said,
"to see where the reach of Christ and the Virgin
converge, and you will learn of the pinnacle
of God's plan for our lonesome and troubled lives."

3.

Still, I never had the slightest inkling
how the system worked until I found
myself on a veranda deep in summer
where something green laced its tendrils
through the trellis behind her.
A crescent of lime was all

that was left in an abandoned glass.
The party had thinned. Were we figures
in a Vermeer much would have to be done
over again: the accuracy of passion called
into question, the woolen hue of a thick
summer night thinned to a crystal brilliance,
obsessions bleached. In such a scene,
eternity seems more than an order
of captured light, it can slip the frame
and sprawl on the floor where the sun
lies quartered by the paned window.
But that night, nothing more timeless
than the laws of perspective governed our pose:
walking side by side, we held our parallel
lives at bay and moved deep into the deafening song
of the scenery, knowing that all we'd done
and said under the common burden of our years
would vanish at the point of our convergence.

ABELARD COMPLAINS

Two or three a week, and on the best days
one topping another, her letters come,
the tumble of her script a poor palimpsest
for the woman who several days ago
laid down these words in a faraway place.
Fumbling numbly with each envelope, I wonder
if my absence taught her what hers taught me.
As if for the first time, she is lying
in my hands, and I am unmindful of decorum,
seeing her as once she was, which is all
I know to do when confronted with this:
a crisp white sheet where it's decreed
that what I hold is the best I'll hold for now.
I feast my eyes on her, and begin to read.

FLORA AND MARY

Denounced by her Muslim brother, Flora and her friend
Mary were imprisoned until such time as they might
apostatize or be sold into prostitution. Both resisted,
and both were beheaded in 851. Their feast day is
November 24.

Córdoba. A cleansing rain.
851 A.D., late November
in Spain, Mohammed not yet
three centuries old,
and Abd-ar-Rahman reclines
in golds and native umbers,
watching his men
become the magnificent Moors.

Betrayals are common today:
there's Mary unaware
of the trampling empire
that will make a fortune of her faith,
and there's her friend Flora, stooped
beside her in the middle ground .
between a treacherous brother
and a simple, human cruelty.

Rain pooled on the cobbles
two women walked long ago
as it pools today. That much I know.
November storms my oak,
the wind lopping limbs
from a burrowed and nested trunk,
and then the storm dies away,
and all's quiet again.

But Flora and Mary are losing
their heads. They fall
and splash in the cobbling rain
as silver and gold become

handsome artifacts in shops
along the alley. The ping
of the hammer rises and fades.
And then all's quiet. Again.

ISLE OF SKYE

They say there are seals here, but I have seen none yet.
—Iris Murdoch

Like a dream of passion, it's gone now.
But once we were actually wet in the face
with it, the cold Atlantic froth
in April under the first cerulean sky
of the year. We'd crossed at Kyle of Lochalsh,
the rumor of seals rampant down the dock,
thickening our interest in blunt and speedy shapes:
just once, we wanted it all,
the glamorous wheeling arc of their sudsy backs,
the purgative salt air, the raucous gulls
barrelhousing for bread-balls, the know-it-all
biologist with binoculars—a ship
of fools the seals would never grace.
I think of them often now, schooling
in diamond channels and blue bays, diving down
and bubbling up, on the brink of instruction.

SANCTUARY

Once when I had time on my hands, I headed down south
in October, and I mean *down* south, where the white
of the cotton and the black of the earth
and the handsome horizon conspired
to level my hopes of ever arriving anywhere.
I speak of it now as a place I know well,
though you could ask me how to find it
and I could not tell you other than to say
it was so flat you felt, standing there,
as a child feels who listens
to a story about how the world came to be
a kind or cruel place—
                                     It was all the same
for a rapt moment, just a tall tale
to live by and a flatness so full of comfort
I liken it now to a sanctuary
where goodness was a wing-flash
beyond the levee, and clarity the coming of daylight.
I would go with you there, but I am afraid
we would follow the old story line
and stay forever because it's said
if you stand long enough
in one place in the Delta, and long enough
down there is not long at all, you will likely take root.
Not a joyful prospect, at first, being mired
in one place for the rest of our very lives,
but down south in October, there's goodness
and clarity enough to last a lifetime,
or at least that's what we will see,
hip-deep in tall cotton, the world
one embracing horizon, with time
now on our hands weighing less and less,
and a line of geese slapping lustily down on the river,
which will seem to us by then nothing at all
but another southern comfort.

ACHILLES CRIES

Mired in the broad maw of a lulled war.
Agamemnon: overbearing, insufferable.
And having just taken Briseis away.
So: slaked lust everywhere.
But not by the sea where Achilles is, not there.
There: one kind of hell
When the sea is *heaving,* the sea is *gray.*
An absence, a despair.

Lesson: the *heaving, gray* sea was *endless* then.
As it is now. And there are the dreams.
Of her. Of rage. Of black hulls turned red in the sun. Of lies.
Where Achilles is now he cannot lead his men.
Or so he believes. Or so it seems.
And Achilles cries.

LOVE LETTER

My God, a verse is not a crown.
—George Herbert

This one's no miter,
    Thank God,
      No refining fire
Or musket flash,

No Flanders trench,
    No pound of flesh
    Or flake of ash
From Mount St. Helen's rim,

And doesn't fume
    Or reconnoiter
    Except to say
I'm home tomorrow,

A dribble
    Down the candle.